The Great Promise

Luke I

KARL BARTH

WISDOM LIBRARY
a division of
PHILOSOPHICAL LIBRARY
New York, N. Y.

Translated by Hans Freund from the German
original *Die Verheissung;* by arrangement with
Chr. Kaiser Verlag.

Printed in the United States of America

THE GREAT PROMISE

LUKE I

PREFACE

The Bible lectures which form the content of this little book were given during Advent in 1934 to my former student audience after my formal lectures and seminars had been forcibly terminated. They were stenographically recorded, and I have gone through them. Because I personally like to recall this pleasant epilogue to my teaching activity at the University of Bonn, I am glad to place them also before a wider circle. And I may perhaps use this opportunity to return the greetings of so many people who expressed to me during all these weeks their real and personal sympathy—grateful as I am that the course I took has been so largely understood. In view of the existing problems, many things had to remain unspoken which I would have liked to say publicly so as to explain what had happened. Likewise with regard to future decisions, I must ask those who place some confidence in me to continue believing that any steps I take will be responsibly weighed to the best of my ability, even if I am not in a position to give an account— as I should like—to all who may be concerned.

Bonn, January 7, 1935   Karl Barth

CONTENTS

THE GREAT PROMISE

LUKE I

LECTURE 1

Luke I, Verses 5 to 25 *

We have before us the story of John the
Baptist, the messenger, the forerunner, who is
to prepare the way of the Lord; we are concerned
with Advent which precedes Christmas. John the
Baptist is no independent figure. He belongs
entirely to Christ. There are no independent
figures at all in the Bible—figures who have any
significance of their own apart from Christ. And
what is true for Biblical figures in general is most
emphatically true for John the Baptist: he is only
there to collect and give back the light that falls
upon him from the figure of the one and only
Christ. Thus standing there, being totally dependent, being totally man and sinner, totally
serving, he is at the same time the sum of the
fulfillment of all of God's promises in the Old
Testament and the sum of the fulfillment of all
coming after him in the figures of the apostles and
evangelists preaching the revelation in Jesus
Christ. The Baptist is both prophet and apostle,
and just as prophet and apostle he belongs to
Christ. The beginning of the Gospel of Luke must
not be divided into two parts, a first which has to

---

* The scriptural text used throughout is from the Revised
Standard Version of the *New Testament,* New York: Thomas
Nelson & Sons, 1946.

1

do with John and a second which has to do with Jesus, but both sections are totally concerned with the same: the birth of Jesus Christ. And the birth of John the Baptist belongs to the birth of Jesus Christ.

Let us for a moment dwell on the fact that here is told the beginning of a life, the pre-history of a man, the story of the childhood of John which then is followed by the story of the childhood of Jesus. What is the meaning of this? We know of various childhood stories in Holy Scripture. We have such a story about Moses, about Samson, and Samuel, and some allusion to it in Jeremiah. We hear Paul in the New Testament in the Epistle to the Galatians speak of his existence before he was born. All this appears to point out in principle from the very outset that we do not have before us here human personalities who have become what they are by means of certain creative forces, certain abilities or qualities or efforts of their own, or through some historic constellations. Everything else one can possibly *become*. A man of God one cannot become. Either one is or one is not. To be a man of God is not the result of human energy or skill or profundity, but to be a man of God happens through grace imparted to a particular man. The Bible by relating childhood stories tells us this: the men of whom we hear are what they are totally through the *grace* of God.

Verse 5. *In the days of Herod, king of Judea, there was a priest named Zech-a-ri'ah, of the*

2

*division of A-bi'jah; and he had a wife of the
daughters of Aaron, and her name was Elizabeth.*

In this verse we have a statement about the
descent of John's parents. Both father and mother
belong to the priesthood of Israel. Their whole
life stands within the context of this people's
divine service which dates back to Israel's being
elected and called through the inscrutable will of
God who willed then and there to reveal Himself
to *this* people and to be their God. The basic
occurrence here referred to is Israel's election—
God's having revealed Himself to Israel. Revelation ties in with revelation. The fulfillment which
is spoken of in the story of John's birth and of
Jesus' birth takes place within the framework of a
past promise bestowed through grace.

Verse 6. *And they were both righteous before
God, walking in all the commandments and
ordinances of the Lord blameless.*

These parents, we are told, were "righteous
before God." Apart from the more objective context described, that is a statement about the
parents themselves who now become the special
bearers of a promise which has reached here the
threshold of fulfillment, and to that extent is
already fulfillment. They were both righteous
before God. In Israel, the land of the Covenant,
where the Law of Moses is actually read and
kept, where the words of the prophets are listened
to, and where man responds as the prophets res-
ponded, there man is righteous before God.
Where he does not place his confidence in him-

3

self, not in any respect, neither with regard to what he is commanded to do in life, nor with regard to his fate or that of his people, nor with regard to the fate of his community, nor finally with regard to the ultimate question: How do I stand before God? Where man cannot expect any of these things from himself, but knows that God, the Lord of the Covenant, in his kindness, in his mercy, with his help, with his forgiveness, is the answer to all these questions asked by him or put to him—there man is righteous before God. Whoever lives in this confidence and throws all his troubles all along the way upon the Lord, he is righteous before God. And now the parents are described as walking blameless in the commandments and ordinances. "Commandments" appears to refer primarily to the commands of the active, practical life, "ordinances" to the regulations of the worship service. The thought behind this "walking" is apparently the following: Man is walking his way, and to the left and to the right of his way the commandments and ordinances of God are placed looking at him. They follow him, they accompany him, so that he walks his way between them, surrounded by them, aware of being responsible to them, claimed by them. To walk without blame in the commandments and ordinances means to consider ceaselessly without becoming guilty of an exception: My way is the way in the face of the law of God. He who is righteous before God walks his way blameless in all the commandments and ordinances of the

4

Lord. Here an invisible tie is effective: Whoever knows so much that he can place his confidence in nothing but God's grace, knows also that he cannot forget the law of God. Both issue from the same source. God has spoken. He has given his promise in which we place our confidence; and his commandments which we own have come to us, that is to Israel, to those who belong to this people. These are the parents of whom it is spoken here.

Verse 7. *But they had no child, because Elizabeth was barren, and both were advanced in years.*

Now we learn of a shadow under which their life is placed, of a sorrow which is imposed upon them and which is of much greater significance according to the whole conception of their time than it is today among us: "They had no child." To have children, to have many children is considered in the Old Testament as a special indication of the Lord's blessing. "They had no child."

Verses 8-10. *Now while he was serving as priest before God when his division was on duty, ⁹according to the custom of the priesthood, it fell to him by lot to enter the temple of the Lord and burn incense. ¹⁰And the whole multitude of the people were praying outside at the hour of incense.*

It happened in all the ambiguity, but also in

all the definiteness of the special will of God that he once again set out to perform his priestly function. It might be important for all that follows to look closely at these three verses describing what a priest is and does, as a presage of the whole Christmas story and, therefore, also of the story of John. The priest, the one, in turn, goes into the sanctuary on behalf of the people, the many. And while they pray, he burns incense. And this means that through the prayer of this one the prayers of the many collectedly, as it were, ascend to God. This is God's order. There is no "free," direct way between God and man; there is an order of this way, and in this order one person stands before God for the others. Afterwards, he steps out of the sanctuary and stands in place of God before men as a herald of his word. The substance and the work of a priest consist in this official function. He is the image, the reflection of the work of Christ. Thus he, Christ, stands for us before God and for God before us as mediator. And when we think of John who is not Christ, this figure in the sanctuary reminds us that even Christ himself is not without his Church, not without a community, and within the community not without the official function which preaches reconciliation. It reminds us of how this procedure may alone be repeated, how this course *has been* initiated, but also how the order is *valid:* the order of the *mediator* and of *mediatorship* between God and man, the eternal and the temporal.

Verse 11. *And there appeared to him an angel of the Lord standing on the right side of the altar of incense.*

The angel of the Lord appeared to him. When *angels* appear in the Bible, this means that *God himself* meets man in concrete reality. God meets man in his life, meets him through his messengers. And where his messengers truly are, there is wholly God himself. This becomes quite obvious here.

Verse 12. *And Zech-a-ri'ah was troubled when he saw him, and fear fell upon him.*

Let us be clear about it. We have to do with a man who is righteous before God, as we heard above, who walks blameless in his commandments, with a priest who watches over the relation between God and man. And now when he encounters God—he is frightened. God is alien to him, God is dreadful to him. To be righteous before God and to walk blameless in the commandments and ordinances thus cannot mean that the encounter of God and man was not something *new* again and again for man, and that the fear of the Lord was not again and again the beginning of wisdom. However we may think of it, of this dread before God, whether we may understand it as a creature's fright before his creator who has called him out of nothingness, or whether we may understand it as the fear of a man who realizes that his doings will not pass before God, or whether we understand it as the fear of a

7

mortal being who faces death—however it is seen and understood, the same still remains: fear and fright. And we would do well not to center on *one* of these meanings of fear. It is not due to man's creatureliness, nor his sinfulness, nor his mortality, but totally due to its being *God* whom he encounters. An attitude toward God which is not the attitude of fear and fright would only reveal that a real encounter between God and man did not occur, that the angel did not appear. God and the fear of God cannot be separated.

Verse 13. *But the angel said to him, "Do not be afraid, Zech-a-ri'ah, for your prayer is heard, and your wife Elizabeth will bear you a son, and you shall call his name John."*

Now comes the answer: The angel said, "Do not be afraid, Zechariah!" Man by himself cannot throw off his fear, but God before whom fear befalls us must take it away. When the angel has come to man, then it resounds, "Do not be afraid"! Here we anticipate the Christmas story in Luke 2 where the angel appears to the shepherds and speaks to them in the same words. It would not make sense to hide before the reality of God in order to have peace and not to have to be afraid, but one must stand fast before the reality of the living God at the price of being frightened. This living God will say to us, "Do not be afraid"!

Verse 14. *"And you will have joy and gladness, and many will rejoice at his birth."*

8

Then comes God's answer which Zechariah is now to learn. Your wife Elizabeth will bear a son! The whole weight of the answer thus lies first of all within the personal sphere. God's answer appears (and is!) entirely geared to the personal concern of this man. "Your prayer is heard"! We have not been told that Zechariah has prayed, and yet it is the answer to a prayer which God has heard. "Your wife Elizabeth will bear a son, and you will have joy and gladness." Thus the word of God which necessarily first frightens man is a *sweet* word. Really a word which is intended for *man,* man as he is, who has wants, who likes to live, in this case who quite simply wants to have a son. This son is promised to him, this un-uttered wish is fulfilled. However, God is not merely concerned with you and me, God's kind-ness always is meant for *many.* "Many will re-joice at his birth." It is the word of God with which the Gospel of Luke is concerned, and even if at the beginning everything seems to take place within the context of family life, it is still *God's* story. It applies within a larger context and by fulfilling your quiet prayers, God also has his works done. "Many will rejoice at his birth."

Verse 15. *"For he will be great before the Lord, and he shall drink no wine nor strong drink, and he will be filled with the Holy Spirit, even from his mother's womb."*

These verses are to circumscribe the figure of John the Baptist. John the Baptist is also the pro-totype of man in Advent, the prototype of the

9

prophet and the apostle, the prototype of the witness and the messenger of the word. He "will be great before the Lord." This being great is not found where we usually speak of greatness. As above stated, it is being righteous before God which matters here, something which is hidden. This greatness will surely appear very small to men. John will be called great not because of his qualities or his abilities, but because he is great before God. He has nothing to glory in and nothing to demand; his greatness consists entirely in what he is charged with, charged like a student with his problem, like a carrier with his load, a servant with a command. It is this "charge" which makes him great. Because God has presented him with this problem, this load, this command, and for no other reason, "many will rejoice at his birth." For this problem, this load, this command will bring joy to many, many people because God, before whom he is great, sends them his saint.

And now we hear that John, as God's chosen ambassador, will have his special place in secular and religious history. He will be an ascetic, he will belong to that group in Israel who prepare themselves for special service to God through diverse privations and renunciations. What does that mean here? Evidently in some contrast to being great before God, as described above, it means that this man living very concretely on earth will stand out, will be different by way of that peculiar distinction which then existed in

10

Israel. This special deportment will be his mark. The hiddenness of his being before God will correspond to a very concrete visibleness. Thus he will go his way. The *figure* of John the Baptist preaching at the Jordan in clothes of camel hair is not separable from his hidden *being* before God; it is not something incidental. John the Baptist would not be John the Baptist without eating locusts and wild honey. Of course, he would not be John the Baptist either if he did not fulfill his spiritual charge, if he did not preach repentance. But when the kingdom of God is proclaimed, a sign in the concrete world needs to be set up, something definitive needs to become visible. For the Church cannot be merely invisible in the world, but to its invisibleness corresponds a visibleness, perhaps a very strange, very offensive, very controversial visibleness. Why the Church is raised up out of the other earthly things in just such a way cannot be answered. The answer consists in the commands which God issues to the Church.

Still in his mother's womb he will be filled with the Holy Spirit. God will be with him. God will bestow his grace upon him. This does not mean that he will make him an especially pious or intelligent or moral person. But having given him his order, God will also assist him, he will be with him. Yes, one has to put it in the reverse. It will come to pass that he, God, is there with his Holy Spirit, and John will be allowed to be present and to be filled with the Holy Spirit.

11

Where God is present, there the situation reverses itself; a man's existence becomes a secondary existence, becomes his grateful assistance to the great deeds of God.

Verse 16. *"And he will turn many of the sons of Israel to the Lord their God."*

He will convert? He? To convert, to turn man to himself, to call man in such a way that he listens, that no man can do; that only God can do. That God *does* himself. But though God does it himself, he does not do it without his messengers. And these his messengers, his prophets and apostles, his John the Baptists who are filled with the Holy Spirit, who in no way need to maintain a significance of their own; about them it may and must be said, *they* convert. Yes, indeed, *he* will convert! Has he thus become a channel of divine grace, is grace committed to him? No. It is said he will turn *many*, not all! *Ubi et quando visum est Deo,* where and when it will please God, will his servant accomplish God's own work.

Verse 17. *"And he will go before him in the spirit and power of Elijah, to turn the hearts of the fathers to the children, and the disobedient to the wisdom of the just, to make ready for the Lord a people prepared."*

He will go before the *Lord* in the spirit and power of Elijah, before *him.* Let us remember it is not John to whom all of this refers, but only the Lord! We know who is meant. It will really

12

be the Lord himself who will now appear on earth. And before him goes John in the spirit and power of Elijah. This means that all those figures before and after Christ's birth belong together. They speak in the spirit and power of someone else. There John follows in Elijah's footsteps; what he then did at the dawn of history, is now done by John. He walks before the Lord "to turn the hearts of the fathers to the children and the disobedient to the wisdom of the just, to make ready for the Lord a people prepared." That is the charge, the command. He is not to make them a people of God; this God does himself. He can only make ready for the Lord a people prepared, that is by going ahead of the Lord, he can only prepare the people, oblige them to listen, disconcert them, command them to be at attention, so to speak (not through his skill, but by virtue of his charge). That is all. And in itself that is nothing at all. And yet it will come to pass through the Holy Spirit that he will convert many of the children of Israel. For where this really happens, where a prophet and apostle really is, there the Lord *follows*. Just as John is not without his Lord, so it may also now be said in reverse: where this delegate of the Lord is, there the Lord *comes*. And there he may and should stand as one who *knows* that the Lord comes. This is not up for discussion, but by doing quite simply his preparatory service, he should know that with it he does *everything*. That he is given *authority* not because of his own doing, but because the *Lord* follows him. He knows about the

the Lord will follow (His servant), so that even a minor or preparatory work "is everything".

13

Lord, and this knowledge is the power of his office. This all of us must learn to understand: the Lord *is* coming. At this one thing we must gaze, very quietly, very joyfully. The charge is there, and where it is, and where you believe in it and affirm and grasp it, there the Lord stands before the door. In this confidence we may go out and proclaim the word of God.

This "to make ready for the Lord a people prepared" is further described in words not easily comprehended—"to turn the hearts of the fathers to the children and the disobedient to the wisdom of the just." "The hearts of the fathers to the children"? Here I can only make a proposal. Do not these words point in the direction that if you want to enter the kingdom of God, you must become like children? Those who have a long life behind them must go back to the beginning, to the situation of a child who begins with life anew. That is involved in rebirth. When we have to deal with God, we must again begin with the A; to go to a beginner's school; that is what it means to be a disciple of Jesus.—"And the disobedient to the wisdom of the just." Here we have again something of the *concreteness* of the Gospel. The thing is to bring people together. This bringing together, this unity to which the people are assembled, this is not just any unity, not unity at any cost, but one part of them must give up something—their disobedience—and must enter into the faith of the others. Before this is done there is no unity of the people of God. A unity prior to this would be a lie, and whatever came

14

of it would in no case be a people prepared for the Lord.

Verse 18. *And Zech-a-ri'ah said to the angel, "How shall I know this? For I am an old man, and my wife is advanced in years."*

Zechariah asks for a connecting link. We know from the Bible that it is not always bad if man asks this question. Luke 1:34! But here we learn that this question, this request for a sign is punished "because you did not believe my words." Why just here? This question is not to be answered. The same response of man can be disobedience in one case, obedience in another.

Verse 19. *And the angel answered him, "I am Gabriel, who stand in the presence of God; and I was sent to speak to you, and to bring you this good news."*

The angel presents himself to him. The sign simply consists in *not* giving him any sign, but in having the angel say to him: I am the angel. Where an angel is encountered, there is no alternative. You either listen to the words of the angel, or the verdict obtains, "You did not believe my words." This authority is the first sign that Zechariah is given. He stands before a wall.

Verse 20. *"And behold, you will be silent and unable to speak until the day that these things come to pass, because you did not believe my words, which will be fulfilled in their time."*

This verse is evidently meant as a description

15

of a sign by which Zechariah is to know: This is *it*. God has truly entered my life.

Verses 21-22. And the people were waiting for Zechari'ah, and they wondered at his delay in the temple. ²²And when he came out, he could not speak to them, and they perceived that he had seen a vision in the temple; and he made signs to them and remained dumb.

A curious sign: The man who can no longer talk, who has lost the power of speech! At the moment when the blessed man is expected to speak, he becomes silent. What has happened? Obviously—and that must be at the beginning of the story of the witness—man has failed. Even man under orders, the blessed man. Insofar as his faith fails him, he cannot speak. And even if he spoke ever so much, it would be words, empty words, and he would really be mute. And even if ever so much dogmatics and ethics were expounded: words, empty words! That is the possibility, that is the threat, which accompanies the office of the witness. Let us by no means forget this Zechariah, even if it does not affect us to the extent that we are mute. Perhaps we are the mutest when we are the most eloquent!

Verses 24-25. After these days his wife Elizabeth conceived, and for five months she hid herself, saying, "Thus the Lord has done to me in the days when he looked on me, to take away my reproach among men."

But this threat is not the last word. Zech-

16

[handwritten margin notes, top left:]
Maybe there is in it.
Maybe he Z.
doubted
where Mary
did not.

④

[handwritten margin notes, middle left:]
The scriptural
story begins
in failure—
like Exodus,
or Hanna,
or Elizabeth.

[handwritten margin notes, bottom left:]
Even hidden
failure.

ariah is no longer referred to. Instead, it is his wife Elizabeth who had no share in his anxious question. Because of this she may now be present where the work of God is done. Man has failed; he disgraced himself and must keep quiet. But when we are unfaithful, God is faithful and remains faithful, and what he has promised will be fulfilled. And Elizabeth in her retirement goes her way, hoping for the God who has spoken with Zechariah, hoping: praised be he who comes in the name of the Lord, of the Messiah of God, the Christ of God whose forerunner her son will be.

LECTURE 2

Luke I, Verses 26 to 38

We are now in the midst of the Advent's message, directly at the point where afterwards only one more word can be spoken: the Christmas message itself. To the Advent's story belongs also the story of an Abraham, a Moses, a David. Indeed, to it belongs the whole story of the people of Israel guided within the Covenant which God has concluded between Himself and this people under the grace which he has bestowed upon them. John the Baptist is the last in the line of witnesses who look toward the coming mystery of Christmas. Here, however, is more than all this. More than Abraham, more than Moses, more than David and more than John the Baptist, more than Paul and more than the whole Christian Church; here is the story of the mother of the Lord, the mother of God herself. Here is an event, unique and beyond repetition, an event which is totally without analogies, which stands out of the series of other events at the Advent as much as Mary is a figure absolutely raised above all the other figures of the Advent: **the extreme end of those who have received the**

18

promise and now wait for the Lord. What has happened to the figure of Mary in the Roman Catholic Church is not surprising—that she has been raised next to Christ to a second center, that a special doctrine of the Blessed Virgin was formulated, that in ecclesiastical piety the figure of Mary could put the figure of Christ in the shade. This is not surprising because the figure of Mary is beyond question a special figure in the Holy Scripture. And yet there can be no question either that a very deep misunderstanding has occurred here if it could happen that Mary was raised to such a position and provided with titles which even in the least could imply a competition with Christ. For *particularly* Mary, *particularly* as forming the extreme end in the line of those who have received the promise and wait for the Lord, is characterized unmistakably as human, as a person who is opposite to God, who is in need of grace and receives grace. Particularly with her even if what has been promised to her is surely unique, it becomes unequivocally clear that to receive such a promise means to be *human*. And this implies to have *faith* and totally *depend* on faith, to think in faith, to act in faith. If anyone belongs to us, totally to us, in the depth of human need and promise, it is particularly Mary who is visited by the angel of God and called to occupy such an extraordinary position as she does. Particularly this extraordinary position shows and proves again unequivocally that there is nothing superhuman, no human suitability for God, no qualification for mediatorship. There is only the

19

grace of God which attends to man. If Mary with her whole person is a testimony for the extraordinary dimension of God, it is to be said that this extraordinary dimension is God's *mercy* which concerns itself with man. Can such a figure meet with worse misunderstanding than that which has happened to her in the Catholic Church?

Verses 26-27. *In the sixth month the angel Gabriel was sent from God to a city of Galilee named Nazareth, [27]to a virgin betrothed to a man whose name was Joseph, of the house of David; and the virgin's name was Mary.*

This beginning of the story reminds one of the story of Luke 1:5-25 where likewise the angel Gabriel appears and visits man. Thus far nothing new in principle has occurred. From *our* perspective, to be sure, there is something very new. We are not John, much less Mary. No angel meets us. That angels *appear* is a peculiarity of *Biblical* stories; there God associates with man in this most immediate way. We, however, will be glad that we may listen to God in his word and in his testimony mediated to us through the prophets and apostles. Among Biblical figures Mary stands in the line of the witnesses, in the line of those to whom angels appeared; and to whom hope and expectation were granted. For Mary it will be more than hope and expectation. Our text intimates this even if it has not yet become visible. It might almost appear at first as if the encounter that occurs to Mary is simpler, less significant than the one which Zechariah is allowed to experience. The Temple has been exchanged for Mary's simple house. What is extraordinary happens at an unexpected place and to someone who does not immediately stand out as John's parents do. Only the fact that Joseph may consider himself as belonging to the house of David reminds us of the context, of the unity of divine revelation. Something new does begin, but it begins in complete insignificance and strange concealment. That the scene of the occurrence is no longer the Temple in Jerusalem but a simple house in Nazareth, a place somewhat scorned as a land where Gentiles and Jews are mixed, may indicate the kind of "new" which here begins: the Christian Church. God now speaks to man outside of the holy place. Only in the person of Joseph the tie with the fathers is maintained. Previously in the Old Testament the house of David had been distinguished as the epitome of God's grace which has come to this people and where now also the place of revelation shall be. In other words, that of old is continued and at the same time something new is unequivocally proclaimed.

Verse 28. *And he came to her and said, "Hail, O favored one, the Lord is with you!"*

Here we still stand within the general framework of promise and of Advent. After all, this word could have been said by the angel to some other Biblical figure. Mary by what is here said to her does not stand out yet unequivocally. She is greeted by an angel: *Ave Maria, gratia plena,*

21

as it reads in the Vulgate. The Luther translation gets nearer to the Greek original when it says, *"Du Holdselige!"* You who are blessed through God's favor! Blessed, distinguished by the fact that God has inclined toward you! With this nothing has yet been said about the maiden herself. Not because of her virtue, not for her special piety is she called blessed. But only because the angel imparts this to her, because God through the angel speaks to her, because the light of God falls upon her, illumines and supports her. It is *grace* which marks her out. Not a possession, but a gift which the angel presents to her while addressing her. "The Lord is with you!" But this gift of God, this light which falls upon her is not something which only comes to her from outside without really concerning her, which was not truly God's *acting* upon *her*. Where there is grace, where God condescends to man, is good to man, there something *new* happens to such a one. "The Lord is with you!" This is to say that now there is a real relation between God and you. You are no longer a little drop in the sea, one of the lost creatures as you like to believe; but in great poverty, in great obscurity, in great definiteness, it holds that the *Lord* is with you. With this *everything* good is awarded and assigned to man however he may be. It holds not only externally, but also wholly internally, in his life, that everything has become new, that there is a new man, the man with whom the Lord is. Man does not become God, but he is no longer without God. That is the accomplishment of grace. If what the

22

name "favored one" comprises represents man's *justification*, then these words, "The Lord is with you!" can be understood as the grace of *sanctification*; it implies that this one now belongs to God. In the German text something else is added here: "Blessed are you among women!"—further emphasizing, "The Lord is with *you!*" There is a maiden among the many millions of women and maidens who has been singled out, selected, with whom God plans a special work. This is always so if man is to hear what Mary is permitted to hear, "The Lord is with you!"—that he then becomes selected, separate, an individual who in this particular way never was before and never will be again. For always the occurrence of grace is unique which thus has never been and never will be again. True, it happens within the church, within the body of Christ, but this is the very mystery of the body of Christ that it is composed of such individuals who as individuals meet with grace, who as individuals are singled out.

Verse 29. *But she was frightened* at the saying, and considered in her mind what sort of greeting this might be.*

This verse makes it probable to me that the end of verse 28 has been rightly added in the German text. Why is Mary frightened? Also in the story of Zechariah we heard of this fright of man. It is a necessary fright, a fright before God. This it can only be if it does not separate

* Luther translation, instead of "But she was greatly troubled at the saying."

23

the grace which comes in the church comes to individuals because of the church (in some way) but not from the church or even through the church.

man from God, but if he in his fright, in his fear,
is bound to God; if man then knows himself more
than ever upheld by God and stands up to God
of whom he is afraid. In this case, Mary expresses
her fright in the question: Why does this happen
to *me*, just to me? We all know something about
the mystery of our self, about the ultimate lone-
liness in which we find ourselves. And he would
lead a superficial life who had never been
astounded at the abyss which is implied by the
experience that I am I, that such a one exists.
Again and again there is nothing more astonish-
ing in the world than we ourselves! But now we
see that this is nothing at all when compared
with the totally other experience which concerns
us here: that *I* indeed encounter *God*, that *God*
concerns himself with *me*, and that *God* wants
something from *me*, that *I* am not too small for
it, that *God* needs me. I would say that perhaps
we have not yet understood who God is unless
we know this wonder. How is it possible for me
to be before God, to be a child of God, and (if
I am besides, a theologian, as all of us here are)
to preach the word of God? What kind of greeting is this: "The Lord is with you"? Surely the
abyss of wonder about ourselves can only be
really comprehended if one has stood once before
this other incomparably different abyss, the abyss
of God's grace. For not every fright is fright
before God, is the kind of fright which is found
in Mary, in the whole story of the Advent, yes,
even in the story of redemption. There are many
stages of fright which have nothing to do with

24

what we consider here. When we perceive in Mary this ultimate humility, we must make it quite clear that she *has not made* herself humble, she *is* humble. It is not a device of self-abasement which matters here, but bowing down before God and his word. The cause of fright lies totally on the other side, totally with him who comes to meet us.

Verse 30. *And the angel said to her, "Do not be afraid, Mary, for you have found favor with God."*

The new event commences with this verse. "Do not be afraid, Mary!" This "Do not be afraid" resounds through the whole Bible. "Do not be afraid," is said to Peter, is said at the Resurrection, and in many other passages of the Holy Scripture. "You have found favor with God." What this special favor of Mary is, the following will tell us. But let us stop for a moment with verse 30. This "Do not be afraid" which again sets an end to fear and does not allow it to be the last word is the word of an *angel*. We cannot remove the fear of God. We cannot say to ourselves: God is not only holy, but also just; not only far off, but also near. We cannot survey the nature of God from some neutral place so as to set our minds at rest. And particularly we theologians must be careful not to be over-smart and apply dialectics to God! It would sometimes be better to have the courage for partiality—deplored though it is —until really an *angel* showed us the other side! There is revelation where the *angel* proclaims,

25

"Do not be afraid!" The angel *says* it to be sure, but it is the *angel.* Here is a way along which we can not walk on our own, but must allow him to guide us. If it is said here further, "You have found favor with God," this does not mean within the context of Biblical language that Mary has previously *asked* for favor. Grace one cannot seek, grace one can only find. It is peculiar to such favor that God finds someone who has not sought him, but who turned away from him as once Paul turned away, and who just then heard the word of God and was turned around. The expression "to find favor" also occurs in the Old Testament, and is never the result of an endeavor on the part of man. The good shepherd looks for and finds the lost sheep. This is it. This finding the Bible calls "to find favor."

Verse 31. *"And behold, you will conceive in your womb and bear a son, and you shall call his name Jesus."*

From this verse on emerges that which is special, which is new in the story of the Advent to which also Mary belongs. Now we remain behind. Now we approach the wonder of Christmas. Now we touch upon its center to which we have no further access. Only a mystical theology could here wish to continue with analogies, but the Bible knows nothing about the Savior's being born in our soul, it only knows about the totally unique event of his "outward" birth (somewhat looked down upon by the mystics) which indeed

26

is to lead to rebirth within ourselves, but which as an event stands opposite to our faith as its object. Put off thy shoes from off thy feet, for the place whereon thou standeth is holy ground! "Behold you will conceive in your womb and bear a son, and you shall call his name Jesus." While the name of Jesus is here pronounced for the first time and pronounced in the context of the great promise, the meaning of what preceded it becomes obvious. We have heard of the encounter with God, of the message of God's grace, of being frightened before God, of the angel's comforting words—all this could still be religious experience, self-asserting Christian piety, could be words and words only. All these are still arrows which point somewhere, and everything will depend upon our eyes really looking where they point. And if here at the end of the Advent story the arrows once again become visible as though increased in numbers, we must be clear that even they would point into empty space unless that would come which here does come: "You shall call his name Jesus!"

This is something which theologically as well as practically cannot be elucidated enough, that indeed the whole content of the Bible from *A* to *Z* including everything we call the Christian Church and Christian dispensation absolutely depends on this name Jesus. The *name* is the last thing that could still be said about someone, and everything now centers around this someone himself. Through this "someone," through Jesus, the

27

Holy Scripture is distinguished from other good and serious and pious books. Through Jesus that which in the Holy Scripture is called revelation, is distinguished from what surely can also be said about other great ones, gods and men. By pronouncing the name of Jesus and remembering what this name says, we appeal absolutely to the highest court, that court which can only speak for itself, which we cannot evaluate ourselves, but which stands absolutely for its own right and its own dignity. The testimony of the New Testament is the daring, completely unheard-of undertaking with regard to whatever is said about God and divine things, to say it not in general, not in the form of doctrine and myth, but to say everything by looking at this one point: Jesus Christ. One cannot understand the New Testament unless one understands this uninterrupted relation to this one name, unless one knows the voice which resounds from this spot. If we were to remove the name of Jesus Christ from the New Testament, it surely would still be a very fine book; and yet it would be completely absurd—as absurd as mere predicates would be whose subject is missing. You could then really by-pass this book; for what exclusively gives it its weight is this name.

And now the name as such is not accidental. Jesus means the savior, the deliverer. This tells us that man is lost, that he cannot help himself, but is in need of a deliverer. And he has *this one* for his deliverer, his savior, of whom it is said:

"You will conceive in your womb and bear a son, and you shall call his name Jesus." "To bear a son"—that is a *man*. Not an angel, a spirit, an idea is in question here, nothing ever so high and great, but what is quite simple and concrete both in its infinite mystery and significance: man. "You will bear a son and you shall call his name Jesus." She shall be the mother, and by giving him this name she shall carry out the will of God and set up the sign with this name.

Verse 32. *"He will be great, and will be called the Son of the Most High; and the Lord God will give to him the throne of his father David."*

This does not say he will be such an excellent man that because of it he will be called a son of God, but: He will be so called because he will be recognized for what he will reveal himself, as the Son of the Most High. Both expressions mean something unique in the New Testament. Also in the Old Testament men are sometimes called sons of God; again in the New Testament the faithful are named God's children. If this can happen, it happens in the perspective that there is one who originally *is* what we others indeed can only *become*, who originally is from eternity and who now is revealed in time, in history, in human life as the one who is from eternity: the Son of God. And God "will give to him the throne of his father David." With this is said: He will fulfill the promise which was made to Israel, he will be the Messiah. He will in

29

truth be something completely new, but a kind of "new" which through the grace of God the forefathers already expected.

Verse 33. *"And he will reign over the house of Jacob forever; and of his kingdom there will be no end."*

With this last and highest promise what is said about Christ is this: He will be a king; he will govern as the Lord of a kingdom. The unique significance of the name of Jesus will now become obvious when we confront the New Testament with the question: Is this really *valid,* is this really God's testimony which I may rely upon, which I may hold on to, with which I may live in the Church, with which I dare to enter modern life? Quite simply the answer to this question depends upon our position with regard to Jesus Christ. And this position again you could find concretely described in this verse 33 in its speaking of the kingdom. One could quite simply ask in view of this verse: is Jesus really for me the one who governs me as a *king* does, that means: Under the sign of the name of Jesus is there for me a claim, a command which I not only cannot evade, but which I also know that I could never contradict? (A claim which simply *holds*?) There it resides in the figure of this man who will be called great and a Son of the Most High, very God and very man, with regard to whom we know: we are bound to him. Being bound to him you can surely have many thoughts, but in spite of all thoughts, one thing is established. He will

30

be a king over the house of Jacob *forever*! I can
only raise the question: Do we know anything
about it? Nothing has been said about us; we are
what we are, but whatever we may be, we are
bound. We belong to this house of Jacob, and
whether we like it or not, we must and will be
where its king is. "And of his kingdom there will
be no end." The order which is here set up has
no end, it holds and it will hold. We know also
other kingdoms, the kingdoms of our thoughts
and ideals and dreams, and then the political
kingdoms. Yes, all these kingdoms have their day.
But one thing cannot be said about any of them:
"Of his kingdom there will be no end." If we
knew about this kingdom and its validity, then
we would understand the New Testament, then
we would know what the Church is, then we
would not let the kingdoms of this world frighten
and worry us so much. We then would be joyful
men, very joyful men! We would be young and
become older and old and finally face death, and
would know that whatever may become of us
and whatever may happen in the world: "Of his
kingdom there will be no end." We would then be
comforted men. If they know of this comfort,
then they know what the name of Jesus means
in the New Testament.

Verse 34. *And Mary said to the angel, "How
can this be, since I have no husband?"*

Now comes the question of Mary—how shall
this happen? The more we realize what the name
of Jesus implies—this kingdom that has no end,

this kingdom being set up on earth, and we ourselves being honored with the fellowship of this kingdom—the more urgently we will ask: How shall this happen, how shall this be possible? How can we comprehend it? Whence do we have ears to hear it, eyes to see it? Mary with this question stands representatively at the head of the whole Advent community and of the whole Church. This is *the* great question which we have to ask. We do *not* know how this is to come about. As soon as we abstract the fact *that* it happens, we can only ask, *how* shall it happen? And this we cannot answer. The question regarding the possibility, the practicality of God's revelation is an unanswered question. It can only be answered from the other side: the *angel* speaks with Mary. He does not speak to her of a husband; but into the midst of her life, into the life of this simple little maiden, is placed what is wholly other, the incomprehensibility of God.

Verse 35. *And the angel said to her, "The Holy Spirit will come upon you, and the power of the Most High will overshadow you; therefore the child to be born will be called holy, the Son of God."*

There is no answer, no explanation to Mary's question. As answer there is only—God himself. Where the Holy Spirit is spoken of, there even more God is spoken of. When the Bible speaks of the Holy Spirit, it speaks of God as the link between Father and Son, of the *vinculum caritatis*. This love which unites the Father and the

32

Son makes it possible that there is a Jesus for _{Jews, too}
us, that for us the Son has become man. The
innermost, the very mystery in the eternal being
of God is also the mystery of his love for us. ||
The Holy Spirit will do it. God Himself will make
it possible that there is for us God's grace and
truth. "Therefore the child to be born will be
called holy, the Son of God." From the fact that
there will be something miraculous about this
birth, it shall be known who he is whom you will
bear. The miracle will be a sign for what he is,
does and accomplishes. And by this sign—we
will not be able to by-pass this sign—we will
know who he is.

Verse 36. *"And behold, your kinswoman
Elizabeth in her old age has also conceived a
son; and this is the sixth month with her who
was called barren."*

It is not easy to explain this verse. Most inter-
preters believe that Mary here shall be strength-
ened in her faith by being reminded of what
happened to Zechariah and Elizabeth. It seems
to me—but I am not entirely clear—that in this
verse a side-glance is thrown upon the story of
John, the story of Jesus' forerunner. From the
great miracle one looks upon the small miracle,
from the great sign upon the small sign. There it
is really not a matter of a miracle, rather of something wondrous. From the height of the mountain, as it were, one looks back once more—the
birth of John is included in the birth of Jesus
Christ.

Verses 37-38. *"For with God nothing will be impossible."* [38]*And Mary said, "Behold I am the handmaid of the Lord; let it be to me according to your word." And the angel departed from her.*

The Greek text does not say, "with God nothing will be impossible," but: "It will not be impossible with God every *word.*" Everything that God speaks is also possible. "Behold I am the handmaid of the Lord; let it be to me according to your *word.*" In Biblical thinking, God's *omnipotence* can only be spoken of in connection with the *word* of God. We do not have to seek God anywhere else but in what he tells us. His omnipotence lives and works in his word. His word creates, governs, and supports us. God's omnipotence is therefore concentrated and collected in his revelation. What God's omnipotence really is, we only notice when we do as Mary does, when we grant, concede, agree: "Let it be to me according to your word"! With this we acknowledge that what God has said will be carried out. Thus Mary finally simply merges into the general story of the Advent. It is the *believing* man who acknowledges this. But in this general Advent story of Mary, the Christmas story already lightens up as her particular story. "To a world forlorn Christ is born."

LECTURE 3

Luke I, Verses 39-56

To understand this text correctly, this story
of the meeting of Mary and Elizabeth and Mary's
hymn of praise, we must stop for a moment and
look back to what we have heard thus far. We
have heard a double word of promise. We read in
verse 13: "Your wife Elizabeth will bear you a
son, and you shall call his name John." And we
read verse 31: "And behold, you will conceive in
your womb and bear a son, and you shall call
his name Jesus." Thus the Son of the Most High
has been promised who will reign over the house
of Jacob forever. And with him, even before him,
there is the servant of the Lord, the forerunner,
his messenger, who will go before him in the
spirit and power of Elijah. What is promised is
the kingdom of which there will be no end;
what is promised is this people made ready for
the Lord—evidently the people who shall live in
this kingdom. Both the kingdom and the people
are represented in these two figures so entirely
unlike one another and yet so strictly belonging
together: Jesus and the Baptist. We heard prior
to this in the story of Mary how entirely this

promise stands under the sign of the miracle—and the same is true indirectly also for the story of Zechariah. With God nothing will be impossible: None of the words which he speaks. What matters is that the promise which God makes he also fulfills. He alone fulfills. Then Mary answers, verse 38: "Behold I am the handmaid of the Lord; let it be to me according to your word." And strangely close by stands the figure of Zechariah, the poor man who hears and consents and yet doubts. They belong together—that Zechariah doubting and being punished because of his doubting, and Mary, having faith. They belong together like shadow and light, and yet—we take this from the whole purport of the first chapter—the light of this behavior of Mary falls back upon Zechariah. His doubts, his punishment, while hidden, are received into the comfort, in the clarity, into the hope which proceed from Mary. No, not from Mary, but from the word which Mary has heard and has believed without doubting.

Verses 39-40. *In those days Mary arose and went with haste into the hill country, to a city of Judah, *40*and she entered the house of Zech-a-ri'ah and greeted Elizabeth.*

We might ask: Is what has happened so far "only" *promise?* Do Mary, Zechariah, and all these other waiting figures only look to the future? Can God's promise be a mere word? Yes, surely, one has to *wait*; fulfillment lies wholly in the future; there is *promise* and "only" promise. To have faith and only to have faith is what matters. But wherever there is waiting for *God* and for the fulfillment of *his* word, wherever *he* is the future and the promise, there the word "only" can mean no restriction. There "only" does not mean any lack. For particularly where "only" the promise of God is believed, there God is *present!*

And thus we hear in verses 39-40 of Mary and Elizabeth as recipients of a promise. This in any case can be spoken of quite definitely as a second fact beside the promise, enveloped by the promise: There are *people* now who have received the promise. With this something *new* has happened. Where there are two people, such as Mary and Elizabeth, who have received the promise, something has—yes, we may even say *everything*—has changed; there the *world* has become new. Still things appear as before; the world has not changed at all: there is still loving and hating, still killing and dying. One might almost ask where could the world appear more an old, a really old world than just here where there are people who have received the promise? Two women, one young and one old, two insignificant, unknown creatures, feeble, not at all equal to the whole problem of human kind, of the nature and character of this world and its forces, its powers and its demons! What is little Mary here for? And what is old Elizabeth here for? Let us keep the question open. Yes, what are they here for, what good does the promise do to them? What good

37

does it do to the world? Nothing, nothing at all, except that while we say nothing has become different, yet secretly, quite secretly, a *new* creature is already provided for. And now we realize how from the very first when these people are presented in the Bible, it is made explicit that these two, these little women, belong together. Now Mary must set out on her way. "In those days she arose and went with haste into the hill country to a city of Judah and she entered the house of Zechariah and greeted Elizabeth." Let us not by-pass this picture. Mary and Elizabeth belong together not only because they are related, not only because their outward lot now appears to be a similar one, but in virtue of the unity of the received promise, in virtue of the necessity of grace which they have found in God. They *greet* one another. This is a greeting, an incomparable greeting between those who recognize one another as both having received God's promise! How are these people united! What is all acquaintance and kinship, all fellowship and love as is otherwise usual among men compared to the greeting occurring here between Mary and Elizabeth? That is what belonging together and being together means in the *Church*. The Church is wherever two people—and now it does not matter at all what kind of people they are—where insignificant people, two simple women, thus belong together and are together in the hope given to them through the word of God and spoken in their hearts. In this hope there is the presence of what is hoped for.

38

Verses 41-45. *And when Elizabeth heard the greeting of Mary, the babe leaped in her womb; and Elizabeth was filled with the Holy Spirit* [42]*and she exclaimed with a loud cry, "Blessed are you among women, and blessed is the fruit of your womb!* [43]*And why is this granted me, that the mother of my Lord should come to me?* [44]*For behold, when the voice of your greeting came to my ears, the babe in my womb leaped for joy!* [45]*And blessed is she who believed that there would be a fulfillment of what was spoken to her from the Lord."*

What do these verses tell us which merely in their outward form strike us as odd in the peculiar realism with which matters are articulated which otherwise are not so articulated? The leaping of the babe in her womb? Why is this told? Why *must* it be told? Why is there no hesitation, why is just this topic so freely displayed: two pregnant women, two expectant mothers? The answer is that where there are such people who have received the promise, such a Mary and such an Elizabeth, where the *Church* is, there is what is called pregnancy in physical life, there is expectancy and the presence of what is expected; there is not only a knowledge of grace, but there is grace itself. Where the Church is, there is he in the midst of them, there is he who is the hope of the Church, without whom there would be no Church, as little as the world which God has created from nothing. Mary greets Elizabeth, and Elizabeth's babe leaps in her womb. That means that here in Mary who greets Elizabeth there is

Sig. of pregnancy and of the leaping in the womb

not merely pledge and promise, but the promised one is actually present, the Savior, the Son of the Most High who will rule over the house of Jacob forever. Where promise is, there is already fulfillment for those who have received the promise; there is not only a "not yet," but also a "here and now." And the whole truth of what will be when the child will be born, when it will live in full view of men, this whole truth is valid even now in all its force and actuality. For this reason the other child leaps in Elizabeth's womb; for this reason even now John the Baptist rejoices and testifies to the Messiah as his prophet and apostle. One would ruin everything if one would say that this is a figure of speech or a symbol. The Bible does not mean it figuratively and not symbolically. Everything depends on our literal understanding of this passage. Where Mary and Elizabeth *are*, there *is* the Savior and there *is* God. There man is blessed through the power of the Holy Spirit. There is also John the Baptist with his preaching, his word of the kingdom of God which is near at hand, with his hairy garment, the man who points to Christ: "Behold, the Lamb of God who takes away the sin of the world." And who must say with regard to him: I am not the light, but I have come to bear witness to the light. I stand like the friend of the bridegroom in front of him who has the bride. All this is present and secretly already happens where these two women, these expectant mothers, meet one another. The Savior is there and John greets him in his mother's womb as surely as it is the work and deed of God. And

40

now the whole being together of these two people
can only be understood from this perspective, and
every word of Elizabeth is a word which she
speaks out in the name of her son John with
regard to Christ. For this reason Mary is blessed
among women, because the fruit of her womb
is blessed. Therefore Elizabeth, the older one, is
so humbly alarmed at the visit of the young
woman. "Why is this granted to me that the
mother of my Lord should come to me, for behold
when the voice of your greeting came to my ears,
the babe in my womb leaped for joy. And blessed
is she who believed that there would be a fulfillment of what was spoken to her from the Lord."
Where people who have received the promise
are together, as are here Mary and Elizabeth,
where the Church is, there is meaning and truth
in what unites these people; not in what they do
together, not in their speaking and thinking,
their being touched in their hearts, not in their
weak attempts to pray together and to praise
God, but behind all of this, (certainly not without
all of this) there is still in the background, still
hidden: Jesus Christ and John the Baptist. That
means there is the word of God spoken by God
himself in the midst of the fear and poverty of
our lives; and there is John, the proclamation of
this word through men. There is the life of faith
as we can live it, the incomprehensible *miracle*
of faith that we can not attain on our own, that
only can be given to us. There is this mysterious
happening: God who concerns himself with man,
and man who gratefully and fearfully attempts

The meaning
and truth
of the Church
is the pre-
sence of
Jesus in it,
and more
pointing to
Jesus.

41

to serve God, this happening which is the mystery of the Church: always Christ and Christ again, and with him John the Baptist pointing to him.

The verses 46-55 contain the Magnificat, the *song of praise* of Mary which Luther has expounded in such an incomparable way. What is this song of praise to do in this place? I think we understand it best when we understand it as an answer to what Elizabeth has last said to Mary in verse 45. Because Elizabeth has said this, it *must* be answered with what Mary answers in her song of praise. What does Elizabeth say in this verse? She says: You *are* blessed while you have believed. Who believes the word, he is blessed in that the word will be fulfilled, will be consummated. There is such a faith as Elizabeth speaks of where now the word in all its fullness holds, where it is read and acknowledged as valid word, although fulfillment has not yet come, the word which needs to be seized upon as *word* and believed; where the "not yet" is outshined by the "here and now," because it is in the "not yet" that the power of God himself lies, not the power of him who believes, but the power of him in whom faith is placed. The relation of Christmas to Advent is in question. Blessed are you who have *believed*, that is *Advent*. Blessed *are* you, that is *Christmas*. Where Advent really is, there is also Christmas. How could it become Advent if there were not Christmas, yes, if Christmas had not been? We hasten from Christmas to Christmas. Where John really is, there is also Christ. And

Christ is never without John. Where Christ is, there is his Church. This Elizabeth has articulated. And now Mary *answers in the name of the Church*, now in Mary herself the Church speaks and says what is to be said where this happening applies to Christmas and Advent, where this secret truth holds, the truth of the presence of Jesus Christ and his messenger. Where this holds, there all men must say together what the song of praise of Mary says, there every individual in this Church must say just this for his own person and his own life.

Verses 46-47. *And Mary said, "My soul magnifies the Lord, ⁴⁷and my spirit rejoices in God my Savior."*

These two verses evidently belong together. "My soul magnifies the Lord, and my spirit rejoices in God my Savior." These first two verses of the song of praise speak of *man*, what his relation to God is, how God is present in his Church. Let us be clear. With this there is at once proclaimed that a miracle has happened to me, or as Luther says, it is a work of God where this happens that the soul magnifies the Lord. We would not really know the Lord if we found it natural that *we* magnify the Lord, that our *soul* magnifies. When we look at ourselves we can only say that we must be infinitely ashamed, for if we, if our souls magnify anyone, then certainly not the Lord but ourselves! However, if it is true that we may speak in the Church like Mary, we cannot do this without revering the pure work of God

[handwritten margin note: Mary in Mag. speaks for all of us (each of us) in the Church; cf. Hannah. The not-yet that is present in (and for) each of us.]

43

that happens to us, a work that we cannot comprehend and in which we do not recognize ourselves. It is a word of the *virgin* Mary who has become a mother not in the way in which a maiden usually becomes a mother, but through the Holy Spirit, through the miracle. Thus it is always a miracle when God, as he does in the Holy Scripture, concerns himself with man, and when man can say: "My soul magnifies the Lord!" It is always a reflection of the virgin birth which then falls into our life, not less miraculous than was the immaculate conception: a work of Jesus Christ, a work of God and not a work of man. For what does it mean to magnify the Lord? Do *we* really need to do this? He, the Most High, is in no need of being magnified by us, but the Holy Scripture tells us that, nevertheless, this is God's condescension out of his love for us, that he thus wants to come to us, that he is extolled through us. And that this at the same time is the favor which we may experience: I may extol God. *Magnificat anima mea Dominum!* And God *wants* to be extolled within our wretched human life. Also that is true in God's infinite love and condescension, infinitely true. And when we ask what this extolling of God consists of in our life, then under the guidance of the Holy Scripture we must say: It is something quite simple, something quite insignificant looking and yet infinite, to be understood only as a miracle. It is simply this: that in our short existence throughout the days and years and decades during which our life is given to us, throughout the worries and prob-

44

lems and struggles of our lives, we are again and again at every step called upon to let God *be* the *Lord*. Why? Because he is God, not for any other reason. Not because we could do anything with him, not because we consider it as useful, but simply because he, God, is the Lord. Let him, God, be the Lord. Let him be in our thoughts, in our inner life, in our conscience. This simple relation: He *is* God the Lord, and he wants now to be this in my life; and I can let him *be* the Lord in the little and the big steps of my life. That could mean to extol God. That would say, "My soul magnifies the Lord!" Then he is for us what he is in himself. That is his grace that it is not too small for him to be also your and my God and therefore to be also magnified by us. For this, however, God must further be my *Savior*. It must be quite clear that when we mean the work of God, we do not mean an ultimate, uncanny force which we perceive somehow and somewhere, neither do we mean destiny which holds the world together like an iron band; nor do we mean one of those ideas by which we comprise what is the highest value to us, what is best, what is highest, the Beautiful, the True. Of all these gods we could not say, "My spirit *rejoices* in him." We can only rejoice in him whom we call God, my Savior. That means him who has come to help us and by his very presence tells us that we are in need of help. Whatever the case may be with everything else: *He* is the one who *helps* us, who takes *care* of us, who brings forth *wholeness* in the midst of the unwholeness of our existence.

45

That is God the Savior. And in this God we can and must rejoice. About the other gods we may reflect, we may bow gloomily to fate, we may pursue our ideas in self-made comfort and fanaticism. But where is *joy?* Joy is the most rare, the most scarce commodity in the world. We have enough of fanatical zeal and enthusiasm and humorless fervour in the world, but joy? That is an indication that knowledge of the *living* God is rare. In God my Savior when we have found him or when he has found us, we rejoice, says Mary. The Savior will always be he who finds us at the end of our way, at the end of our scramblings and our flights, at the end of our optimism and pessimism. There where we only know one thing, that is this: I am lost unless he helps me.—So much about man before God in the Church.

Verse 48. *"For he has regarded the low estate of his handmaiden. For behold, henceforth all generations will call me blessed."*

What now follows will be a statement about *God.* "He has regarded the low estate of his handmaiden." Here is shown the reason why it happens that my soul magnifies the Lord and my spirit rejoices in God my Savior. This does not happen because of some independent, self-made elevation of soul, but because he, the Lord, has *regarded little* Mary, because he, the Lord, has *regarded* his *poor* Church. Look at little Mary, look at the poor Church; there is no reason for elation and joy. But contemplate him to whom both Mary and the poor Church look, then you

46

understand it. What has happened? He has regarded the *low estate* of his handmaiden. Thus
it is clear that God is a God of the poor, a God of
those who are in need, who are there beneath,
deeply, deeply beneath. How should it be otherwise if he is the Savior? But just because of this,
that he regards the low estate of his handmaiden,
he shows himself as a gracious God; as he who is
good to us with a kindness which presupposes
nothing, which knows the condition we are in
and yet which comes to our aid. This God we
need; that is truly God who regards the low
estate of his handmaiden, only regards. How
beautiful this is. It is only required that God
regards us, turns his eyes upon us. There is also
between us the mysterious moment when we
look into one another's eyes in order to say
to each other: I do not want to hide anything
from you, but I will show myself to you as I am.
There you *have* me. Nothing else is needed before
God, but that he regards us; that is all. In this
there lies the mystery of the virgin birth; there is
the presence of God. And everything which comes
afterward is included in what looks so insignificant: "He has regarded the low estate of his
handmaiden." "For behold, henceforth all generations will call me blessed." It is powerful how this
stands here side by side: the one which is so
insignificant that it requires only to be *regarded*
by God in order to have the fullness of grace
poured out; and now the power, the significance
of this event: "All generations will call me
blessed!" All angels of all heavens now only look

47

at this one place where this Mary is, and yet, nothing has happened to her but that God has regarded her low estate. This short moment is full of eternity; there is nothing greater between heaven and earth, and if ever in world history anything important has happened, it is this "regarding." We speak of Mary, but we also speak of the Church at the same time, and we speak of ourselves too. It is not as can be seen on those touching certificates of confirmation that like a little girl we must carry through the dark a small candle which a gust of wind can blow out at any moment and which we must protect with our hand, no: "Behold, henceforth all generations will call me blessed." There is no trembling and hesitating, there you *know*, there definite affirmation has been won. The beginning and the end of world history and its center look at the one point, at Christ. We are called upon to take our stand next to Mary and to see that this rejoicing and this extolling of the soul can and may be any moment our own rejoicing. We must only allow for what she allowed for: "Let it be to me according to your word!"

Verse 49. *"For he who is mighty has done great things for me, and holy is his name."*

These great things are once again the very simple things, the very secret things. The things which consist in this being *true*: Immanuel, God with us! He who is mighty and whose name is holy! How does it happen that I have contact with God's almightiness and with God's holiness?

That he has done such great things for me? Must man not perish when God concerns himself with him? What is man and the holiness of God? We think of Isaiah: "Woe is me, for I am undone!" And now it says, no, not being undone, but peace, joy, gratitude—"He has done *great* things for me." Here is incomparably more than in Isaiah. Here is that reality which Isaiah has beheld. Here is God who has himself become man. One should think humanity could no longer persist since Christ is there, since he has entered into time. But now it is just the reverse. It *can* persist, it *may* persist, because he is in the midst of us. He safely leads us to the land of Canaan if we only let him do so. For everything which then happens to us when we let the Lord really be the Lord, these are then great things. It is a whole kingdom that is placed into our hands but for our wanting to be small, that is wanting to be great outside of him.

Verse 50. *"And his mercy is on those who fear him forever and ever."*

Here the word "mercy" is to be stressed as an explanation of what was referred to as "being regarded" in verse 48, and the "great things" in verse 49. Just this is mercy. In the Church one knows that this is not merited, that God does not owe us anything, not even that he regard us. Naturally it might be expected that God should no longer want to have anything to do with us.

* Luther translation, instead of "And his mercy is on those who fear him from generation to generation."

49

That he regards us, this comes from his "kind heart," from the miracle of his divinity which is love. "And his mercy lasts forever and ever with those who fear him." Let us take notice of this "forever and ever," this further and further. Such a "Mary" does not have to be blown up gradually so that she would no longer be in need of mercy. No, your *mercy* lasts forever and ever with those who *fear* him. *His* mercy, not a mercy as we practice it. His mercy is new every morning. Progress in our life can only consist in my understanding a little better every day that I am greatly in need of God's mercy; and when I am at the end of my glorious life, then I will have to say with finality: Now I am undone unless I find mercy. And if God then granted me another day, this last day would only tell me once again: I am dependent on grace. This would be progress, real progress! For just by clinging to God we let him be true. To this "forever and ever" of divine mercy would have to correspond a "forever and ever" of our approach to the Divine Throne and of our bowing to his mercy.

Verses 51-53. "*He has shown strength with his arm, he has scattered the proud in the imagination of their hearts, ⁵²he has put down the mighty from their thrones, and exalted those of low degree; ⁵³he has filled the hungry with good things, and the rich he has sent empty away.*"
What is said here does not merely concern God's acting upon individual men, but here is proclaimed quite briefly what God's order in the

world means, how from the perspective of the Church things on the whole are going: what is valid and established, what we may expect with confidence, but of what we must also beware because it holds and stands and is a law of all existence. Where the Church is, where a Mary and an Elizabeth are, where the Savior has come and with him also John, there one knows that "He has shown strength with his arm." And this is really the secret of our life, also of our social life, also of world history, of cultural history, of religious history. The *arm* of the Lord: Luther and Calvin agree that it means the work of the Lord in so far as it takes place in our life and in the world entirely without the aid of a creature. God also acts through creatures, but God does not only act through them, he also acts purely through himself, quite wondrously, as *God.* He does not need the creature for his work. And woe to us if we should close our eyes before such a happening. He himself, he personally acts, to be sure, in the *world*, that is within the human sphere of action, but entirely after his, not after man's order: *God* as man. Where his word is, there is *God* as man; there is this God's strength although it happens on earth and among us men. The arm of God is the word of God, and the word of God is the son of God. And through his arm God shows strength, that means he governs. That is what matters, and this we are summoned to when we are in the Church, that we cheerfully and confidently look out at the ocean of life and of history in quiet and simple trust. "He shows

[margin handwriting: the arm of the Lord]

[margin handwriting:] special sense]

[margin handwriting: the church does not participate in this power. It is called to trust it, Mary is the model.]

51

strength with his arm." He sustains all things through his word. And that means, "He has scattered the proud in the imagination of their hearts, he has put down the mighty from their thrones." That is: Nothing can persist in the world that wants to be a power, a force, a dignity of its own without the arm of God. It is characteristic of the play-acting of human life, not only of the mighty events of world history, but also of every single life, that we again and again ascend thrones in order to be the mighty ones. One can do this very efficiently, very genteelly, very ingeniously, and yet one wants to be mighty aside from the power of the word. But: "He has put down the mighty from their thrones and exalted those of low degree." We are exalted and our soul will only exalt the Lord if we are of low degree. God has nothing to do with the mighty ones. All of us, probably, are such mighty ones and must be put down from our thrones if we want to have anything to do with God. How does God do this "putting down from the throne," and how will it become true also in world history? How is it that this is the final truth also with regard to what happens among men? We need not think of something big and loud and external. The Savior is not a destructionist (as Blumhardt once said) who goes through world history like a roaring lion. God's ways are always *hidden*, quiet ways. What happens here is not dramatic, but all the more wondrous. It is only required that God turns away, does *not* consider us anymore as he regarded Mary. Being put down from our thrones

52

quite simply happens, I believe, in this way—
that God turns away from us—and that is the
most terrible thing that God can do to us, simply
to let us proceed. From our point of view it can
simply mean to have arrived at the top rung of
the ladder. This would be the downfall when I
perceive that at the end of my career, of my
untiring climbing, I have become what I wanted
to be; it is achieved, but achieved without God.
That is the most terrible hell when *our* planning
succeeds, *our* goal is reached. Let us not by any
means imagine hell as a place where one is
permanently beaten or roasted. There will be
gathered indeed great lords and nice people, but
great lords and nice people without God. Who
now may persist in what they *wanted* in life and
have *attained*, must persist from eternity to eternity. That is damnation and that is hell, and well
for us if God does us the favor of making us
aware in time of the kind of journey on which
we are bound. He is concerned with those of low
degree who have understood that in their low-
liness they are in need of the Savior and are *grateful*. Not in vain is this *law* included in Mary's
song of praise. It is also a praise of God.

Verses 54-55. *"He has helped his servant
Israel, in remembrance of his mercy, [55]as he
spoke to our fathers, to Abraham and to his
posterity forever."*

Mary returns at the end of her song of praise
into the line of all those who belong to the
Advent; now she is again simply a member of

her people, Israel. She says, God has remembered his mercy and now fulfills what he has promised to his people. His mercy has no end.—

As Mary and Elizabeth lived in the *promise,* so do we with them, and for this reason we also live in *fulfillment.* This seems to me to be the meaning of this song of praise; the Church speaks the words with Mary, no, *in* Mary: "My soul magnifies the Lord," and further: "He has regarded the low estate of his handmaiden," and still further: He is the God who "has shown strength with his arm" and who "remembers his mercy."

LECTURE 4

Luke I, Verses 57-80

May I begin with a comment on the division
of the chapters. This division is not originally
found in the New Testament, but was made
later. And I would like to say at this point that
the story had to be divided just the way it has
been thus far, namely that everything up to now
is the first chapter, and that the second chapter
begins with the birth of Christ. At first sight the
question could be raised: Would it not have been
more meaningful to begin with the story of the
promise and the meeting of the two mothers
and contrast it with the fulfillment of what was
promised? But no, the birth of John is separated
from the birth of Jesus although it too belongs to
the fulfillment. Indeed, what we hear at the end
of our chapter and as continuation of our thinking
about the Advent: the birth of John and what
occurred at his circumcision, and the speech of
Zechariah, all of this is surely fulfillment; and
yet it is even in fulfillment still Advent, still expectation. It is still John and not yet Christ. And
although Christ does not come without John,
although Christ is totally unthinkable without this

witness of his, although John belongs to Christ, yet we must not forget—and the chapter division indicates it unmistakably—there is still man, one who is totally as we are, not Christ, not the son of God. There stands man in the midst of the redemption story, received and accepted; but in so far as he is man and only man, the fulfillment of the birth of Christ is in contrast to him something new, something different, something incomparably greater.

Verse 57. *Now the time came for Elizabeth to be delivered, and she gave birth to a son.*

Outwardly this appears the same as in chapter 2, verses 6-7 where the identical account is given of Mary. The same event and yet a difference like that of heaven and earth, of God and man—but of God and man who have *found* each other, who now have become one, a difference of God and man which is opposition no longer. We must see both: the unity of Christ and John, of God's word and his witness, and the distinction between both. The unity of Christmas and Advent and the double meaning necessarily contained in it.

Verse 58. *And her neighbors and kinsfolk heard that the Lord had shown great mercy to her, and they rejoiced with her.*

They rejoiced with her, with this old woman, this Elizabeth to whom this unexpected purely human joy is given, this so humanly pleasing experience: that she may still become a mother completely unexpected as it was from what could be humanly foreseen. When a man of God is born, an Isaac, a Samson, a Samuel, this is always weird, always something unexpected, surprising, something astounding. Here it does not say that the neighbors and friends heard that joy had befallen Elizabeth, but the Holy Scripture speaks at this point of God's mercy, "that the Lord had shown great mercy to her." That is the mystery of such an event where man experiences joy and perceives joy; that is the secret truth: God is merciful. Something of the infinite wealth of Divine kindness has fallen into this human life, and where man looking at it from the outside is astounded at a happening such as occurs on earth and among men, there it is truly to be said: *God* has acted. It is an external aspect to which this internal one corresponds. And they "rejoiced with her." At first this is to be understood as simply human. Is there something else hidden in this joy which has to do with the *mystery*? That would be a Christmas joy if we could give this to each other—that someone else is faring well and that we may participate in it as in a gift of God. The mystery of God's mercy and the joy about this mercy would surely remove everything that we still foster as Christmas-sentimentality. Human life is in reality a serious and sober matter and is totally in other hands than our own. If we know this about one another: I am led and the others are led too, then we could begin really to rejoice with each other. And whether we can do that, this will also be the question with which we once again now enter the Holy Season.

What matters in our text is this: A man is born, and this man shall be a witness of God. Such a witness of God, first simply considered as a man with his qualities, his sober bearing, his deep thoughts, the power of his words, the courage of his behavior, the boldness with which he dares to go his way—all this may be counted to the blessing which becomes visible in human existence through the mercy of God. But it is all-important to perceive this—that it is God's *mercy*, and the rejoicing would have to look away from man to him who has placed man there. *Everything* depends upon God's having sent him.

Verses 59-60. *And on the eighth day they came to circumcise the child; and they would have named him Zech-a-ri'ah after his father, 60but his mother said, "Not so; he shall be called John."*

This is the incident: John is to receive his name at the circumcision. His father who cannot talk cannot participate in this act. They named the child after his father Zechariah. Thus it is ordered so that the life of the family, of the blood, of the tribe, remains triumphant, an idea well pleasing to God. In this way things are to take place. And now strangely enough the mother interferes, and in spite of all that we might expect from her, proclaims her: "Not so; he shall be called *John!*"

Verses 61-63. *And they said to her, "None of your kindred is called by this name."* 62*And they made signs to his father, inquiring what he* *would have him called.* ⁶³*And he asked for a writing tablet, and wrote, "His name is John." And they all marveled.*

A great shock for the family! "None of your kindred is called by this name." Not at all in the order of things as ordained. Where does this unusual name come from? What is now to happen? They beckon to the father. Then the wholly unexpected occurs; the father completely sides with Elizabeth in this question and declares quite categorically: "His *name* is John." There is no discussion. Unequivocally it is written on the tablet. "They all marveled." When this break-through ensues through Elizabeth and Zechariah themselves, when what is quite unexpected takes place with this unusual name contradicting all tradition, it has evidently this meaning: Where God has placed a witness, a man of the Advent in contrast to the Messiah and as his messenger, where a man is called upon to be a man of God and a prophet, there this is not simply an event in a series of other events. That which calls this man out and makes him a witness has in itself nothing to do with tradition, family, people, or the like. He is surely the son of his father; the order of creation is not destroyed; what is God's command remains valid. But if this child stands under a call, this cannot be explained by his being the child of his parents. And if the child is a witness, this does not point to anything that his father or his mother could ever do for him. For within the frame of his old birth a *new* birth has taken place. Then the traditional name can

59

no longer be authoritative, then a new name must be found. Something takes place in this life, within this area of human existence, which could be compared with the building of the tabernacle in the desert or the building of the temple on the mountain rock at Jerusalem, something that in this way had not been expected and that is now simply present as an extraneous substance. Nature is not destroyed, history is not interrupted; but within natural, historic human life wherever God acts upon man, there is nothing that could claim dignity of its own as against the aggressive, justifying and valid words of God. But what is natural and historical is now entirely acted upon by the word of God, is wax in his hands which is molded—clay in the hand of the potter. And if it is not destroyed, this does not mean that over against the word of God we could set up as our own doctrine what we are and believe as men. All this must be thrown into the fire like iron. Of course, it remains iron, but it will lose its form, it must be purified in the heat, must become liquid and receive a *new* form. And therefore: not Zechariah but John. And so far there are only these two people who proclaim it over against the whole of society, which believes that everything remains as it was before.

Take notice that it is Elizabeth who proclaims it first when she somewhat abruptly begins to speak: "Not so." She understands and sees through the situation and is not perturbed by the authority of a family order. It is not to go unnoticed that it is first *Elizabeth.* It is a very

60

peculiar thing about the *woman's* role, just in the first chapter of Luke, a very notable and honorable role! And if it is under discussion whether a woman should have a part in preaching the gospel, such a discussion would have to be preceded by a very thorough exegesis of this chapter before one should be allowed to answer conclusively with reference to I Corinthians 14. Neither Mary with her song of praise nor Elizabeth with her "Not so!" have kept silence. They have *said* something very decisive in the community and with the community of all time.

When Elizabeth acts in this way, and afterwards also Zechariah, it is not the belief of the text that they could have done it on their own. It might look that way at first sight, and people might think and say: How original! But originality must not be confused here with that which a man does because he must do so, because the Holy Spirit speaks through him. It must be clearly presupposed in connection with the text and representing the view of the text that the two people are filled with the Holy Spirit. Elizabeth dares to make this interference as the mother of that John who is filled with the Holy Spirit already in his mother's womb. And the same applies to Zechariah, still suffering under the punishment for his unbelief—he is still mute—when he nevertheless gives a sign such as he being mute can give. He writes, "His name *is* John." Zechariah does so because the light is already upon him of which we hear in verse 67: "His father Zechariah was filled with the Holy

Spirit." What happens now happens in the truth of this future event.

Verse 64. *And immediately his mouth was opened and his tongue loosed, and he spoke, blessing God.*

What Zechariah did according to verse 63 is simply an act of obedience. He remembers what he was told and does it. His obedience and the presence of the Holy Spirit cannot be separated. In the beginning Zechariah was not quite willing to obey. Now he obeys because God has kept his word and given him a son. If only we had this Zechariah type of obedience so that at least we would believe and obey in view of divine fulfillment occurring before our very eyes! And now it happens that the punishment is taken from him while he is obedient. He can talk again. Not because he is obedient, but because God fulfills his promise. Something out of the ordinary has happened. These old people have received a son. In view of this merciful deed of God it is a matter of course that Zechariah obeys and does so quite unobtrusively. He simply sits there and writes on a tablet. Something quite insignificant, but this is his obedience. On the other hand, where God shows his goodness he can remove punishment which is due to unbelief. Be assured that when you do not really obey, then you are *mute* and have *nothing* to say. But at the moment when unbelief is taken away, then the mouth of man is opened again, then Zechariah can *talk*

62

again. "He spoke, blessing God." His mouth has not been opened for some unnecessary talk, but for the praise of God. I would say that what is here described in the person of Zechariah in verses 63-64 is similar to what happens with Elizabeth. In both cases it is a paraphrase of what John the Baptist will be. As in a silhouette on the wall, we see in what occurs to Zechariah how it happens that a man becomes a witness of God. First this appears impossible since man does not have faith. To be muted happens as punishment. But it becomes possible that a man witnesses for God because God himself is ready in his incomprehensible goodness and fulfills what he promises even if man's faith is weak. God stands by his word, and then even faith becomes possible as a miracle. Then man has the power of speech. How does this come about? We cannot explain it other than to say that it has its ground in God's goodness. Nevertheless, he can indeed speak, and a witness is ready. This is the spiritual birth history of John the Baptist. Dear Friends, we can also say the spiritual birth history of the theologian. Thus it can happen that one becomes a *minister*. Surely it cannot happen in any other way. It is part of the secret of this chapter how the approaching figure of Jesus and of his forerunner are projected in these persons of the Advent.

Verses 65-66. *And fear came on all their neighbors. And all these things were talked about through all the hill country of Judea;* [66]*and all who heard them laid them up in their hearts, saying, "What then will this child be?" For the hand of the Lord was with him.*

These verses describe the impression made upon the neighborhood: a great wealth of human sympathy. But if one adds up what is said by the people it amounts to some great bewilderment changing into fear. That is something that happens very often in the New Testament—that men "are afraid." The Gospel of Mark even breaks off with it. Again and again it seems to be something very much alive, this fear.

It is a delightful question: "What then will this child be? For the hand of the Lord is with him." The matter does not seem to them completely satisfactory. They do not participate in full sympathy—comparable perhaps to one's standing in front of one's neighbor's burning house witnessing a sudden conflagration. What puzzles the world when it is confronted as it is here with the problem of the witness? First it appears as an event as any other, a man as others, who then suddenly steps out of line: not Zechariah but John shall he be called! The world is amazed—and how should it be otherwise—where God singles out a man in this way, elects, "sanctifies," as the Bible says. There is one who is not in the column in which men are accustomed to hold on to each other and march in step, one who goes, perhaps, even a different, an opposite way; he is a cause of disturbance, of great uneasiness for the rest. All of them are suddenly put to the question through this fact and through this

Deviance

64

one person: Where are we really, what are we going to do, if it becomes possible that someone is *thus?* Such a child can be a very dangerous thing. What shall become of the child?. If this happens, something so extraordinary, unassimilable, how shall things go on in the city and country, the state and nation? A single exception rather than confirming the rule makes the whole rule doubtful. Such a sight can mean great joy, hope, expectation. But it can also be that there is refusal, reserve, hatred. And we see this in the life of John and his end. Evidently both can be said. The witness should not be surprised if he fares in the world as does here John the Baptist.

Verses 67-80. *And his father Zech-a-ri'ah was filled with the Holy Spirit, and prophesied, saying, "Blessed be the Lord God of Israel, for he has visited and redeemed his people, ⁶⁹and has raised up a horn of salvation for us in the house of his servant David, ⁷⁰as he spoke by the mouth of his holy prophets from of old, ⁷¹that we should be saved from our enemies, and from the hand of all who hate us; ⁷²to perform the mercy promised to our fathers, and to remember his holy covenant, ⁷³the oath which he swore to our father Abraham, ⁷⁴to grant us that we, being delivered from the hand of our enemies, might serve him without fear, ⁷⁵in holiness and righteousness before him all the days of our life. ⁷⁶And thou, child, shalt be called the prophet of the Most High; for thou shalt go before the Lord to prepare his ways, ⁷⁷to give knowledge of salvation to his people in the*

*forgiveness of their sins, ⁷⁸through the tender
mercy of our God, when the day shall dawn upon
us from on high ⁷⁹to give light to those who sit
in darkness and in the shadow of death, to guide
our feet into the way of peace." ⁸⁰And the child
grew and became strong in spirit, and he was in
the wilderness till the day of his manifestation to
Israel.*

These words of Zechariah are to be understood as a whole, as an explanation of the knowledge which he has of his son, this witness of God
who is given to him. If we look at the content
of this speech and observe that in this song of
praise hardly any reference is made to John,
explicitly only in verse 76, it becomes obvious
that this word about the witness is really a word
about Christ. He is spoken of here in a much
more pronounced way than in Mary's song of
praise. If one wants to speak about the Christian
as a witness, one can only say that man is involved, to be sure, but before and afterward and
in a strict sense only that other one can be spoken
of for whom this child shall be the witness. The
light that a Christian witness carries and that
issues from him can only be a receiving, borrowed
light, derived from the independent, original light
which he can only serve with his existence. All
talk about prophets, witnesses, Christian bearers
of truth, Christian personality, about heroes and
Fathers of the Church can only be meaningful if
it proceeds as does this song of praise of Zechariah; if man remains completely the child about
whom for himself nothing special is to be said.

66

Well for us if this may be said about us men:
"And thou, child, shalt be called the prophet of
the Most High." *You* are not spoken of any further! You are not important at all! Not what
the child is himself, but what he has to say is
important, what through this child is pronounced.
For he is a prophet through whom someone else
is meant to speak. The prophet himself is left with
his gratitude and his prayer in view of him who
has put him there. Jesus Christ, the promised
Messiah, he is the meaning of the event that has
taken place in this family with the birth of John.
He, the God of Israel, "has visited and redeemed
his people, and has raised up a horn of salvation
for us." The joy over the birth of John must be
immediate and direct: joy at the presence of the
Savior. In order to explain who John is we must
think of Jesus Christ himself, and we must further
consider that he is the expected Messiah, that
Jesus has been prophesied. What happens in the
presence of Jesus Christ is nothing new, it is
something of old that always was, and now has
become visible for all time having been established for past and future time as the midpoint.
John witnesses for him; the prophets witness for
him.

"That we should be saved from our enemies."
Zechariah sees the people of God, he sees the
Church in the whole magnitude of its being
menaced by its human enemies—who still are
not its worst enemies. For its worst enemies are
unbelief, superstition, erroneous belief in which
Satan has mixed his seed among the word of

67

God. These are the real enemies. What could the Assyrians, Babylonians, Philistines and Egyptians do against Israel if Israel were true to God? But because it is not true, it sets up its own real enemies, and from these enemies it has been delivered. In this danger God attends to us. In Jesus Christ we are not up against dangers of no consequence. But God attends to us in Christ while we are faced with the danger of not having trust in God and not having courage. In this problem of all problems, he is our Savior and Deliverer. Our deliverance consists in God's making his word come true. Israel does not let it be true and breaks its vow. But God remembers his Covenant, he stands by his word; his word is *his* word, and that is the deliverance. How stupid we are if we consider the word a mere word. Where God's word is, there is *God himself*, in *his* faith in spite of our faithlessness—and in the midst of our faithlessness—his word touches us. Just I am meant, I the faithless, the disobedient one. This man who is not capable of anything, not even of praying, not even of a little bit of praying, he is meant. Thus God has been faithful to our fathers; thus he is faithful to us. He will grant us to live a life without fear in his service. This consolation from the goodness of God which finds us in our lost condition is by its very nature also a claim. God remembers us in our lost condition in order that we may serve him a life-long without fear. That is a *gift*; not a law is established here! This is what forgiveness implies— that God's presence is *given* to us, and that we

68

may live in this presence, that we may *serve* him. We may serve him without fear while fearing only him, therefore without any other fear; even without fear of ourselves, let alone of all others. We may serve God without fear—and do so as a gift—in holiness and righteousness which is pleasing to him. There is a holiness and a righteousness in which one is to ask continuously for the word of God. Again and again to hear, and again and again to receive, for this we are delivered.

And now with regard to the John passage in the midst of the song of praise: to witness, that is your charge. To speak of this helper and redeemer, Jesus Christ, that is the charge, the inexhaustible charge of your life. What will become of you in view of the fullness of what is here to be said if you become what you are here addressed, a prophet of the Most High? In verses 77-79, consideration returns at once to him who shall be spoken of. The knowledge of salvation consists in man's being placed before God, before the merciful God, before the God who forgives our sin. In this mercy God has visited us "from on high to give light to those who sit in darkness and in the shade of death, to guide our feet into the way of peace." We must speak of the function of Jesus Christ when considering the function of the witness who only acts as the messenger who delivers a letter.

With this we have reached the boundary of Advent, of an Advent which is already Christmas. That would signify celebrating Christmas if we let ourselves be invited and called, if we took our position where John stands in his artless humility, but also in his infinite, incomparable greatness, as God's Ambassador.

And now may God grant us all that in this grave critical time we may celebrate Christmas with each other in worshiping the God who has done infinite good to us and the world, as the Gospel says and again says it anew; and that we may enter the New Year not without singing and saying with the psalmist, "O taste and see that the Lord is good: blessed is the man that trusteth in him."